Pakistan's Criminal Folly In Kashmir

The Drama of Accession and Rescue of

Ladakh

`Dr. Wiqar Ahmed of the BBC Urdu service quoted that `the Tribal invasion was a *criminal folly* which sealed the fate of Kashmir'. He was explaning the view in the book "Memories of Jinnah" by his secretary, KH Khurshid. Wiqar was participating in a BBC discussion with Mark Tully and Professor Alstair Lamb on the Kashmir problem on 25 November 1991".

Pakistan's Criminal Folly in Kashmir

The Drama of Accession and Rescue of Ladakh

Padma Bhushan
Lt. Gen. (Retd.) Dr. M.L. Chibber
PVSM, AVSM, Ph.D.
Jawaharlal Nehru Fellow

Manas Publications
New Delhi-110 002 (INDIA)

MANAS PUBLICATIONS
(Publishers, Distributors, Importers & Exporters)
4402/5A, Main Ansari Road,
(Opp. HDFC Bank)
Darya Ganj, New Delhi - 110 002 (INDIA)
Ph.: 23260783, 23265523 (O); 23842660 (R)
Fax: 011 - 23272766
E-mail: manaspublications@vsnl.com
Website: www.manaspublications.in

ISBN: 81-7049-095-2

Second Impression 2008

Rs 495/-

Typeset at
Manas Publications

Printed in India at
Rajdhani Printers, Delhi
and Published by Mrs Suman Lata for
Manas Publications, 4402/5A, Main Ansari Road,
(Opp. HDFC Bank)
Darya Ganj, New Delhi - 110 002 (INDIA)

The gallant and fearless volunteers in Jammu and Kashmir who spontaneously came forward to fight the invaders from Pakistan in 1947 and 48. Their sacrifice, daring dedication and heroic exploits gave birth to the unique Regiment of the Indian Army:

JAMMU AND KASHMIR LIGHT INFANTRY

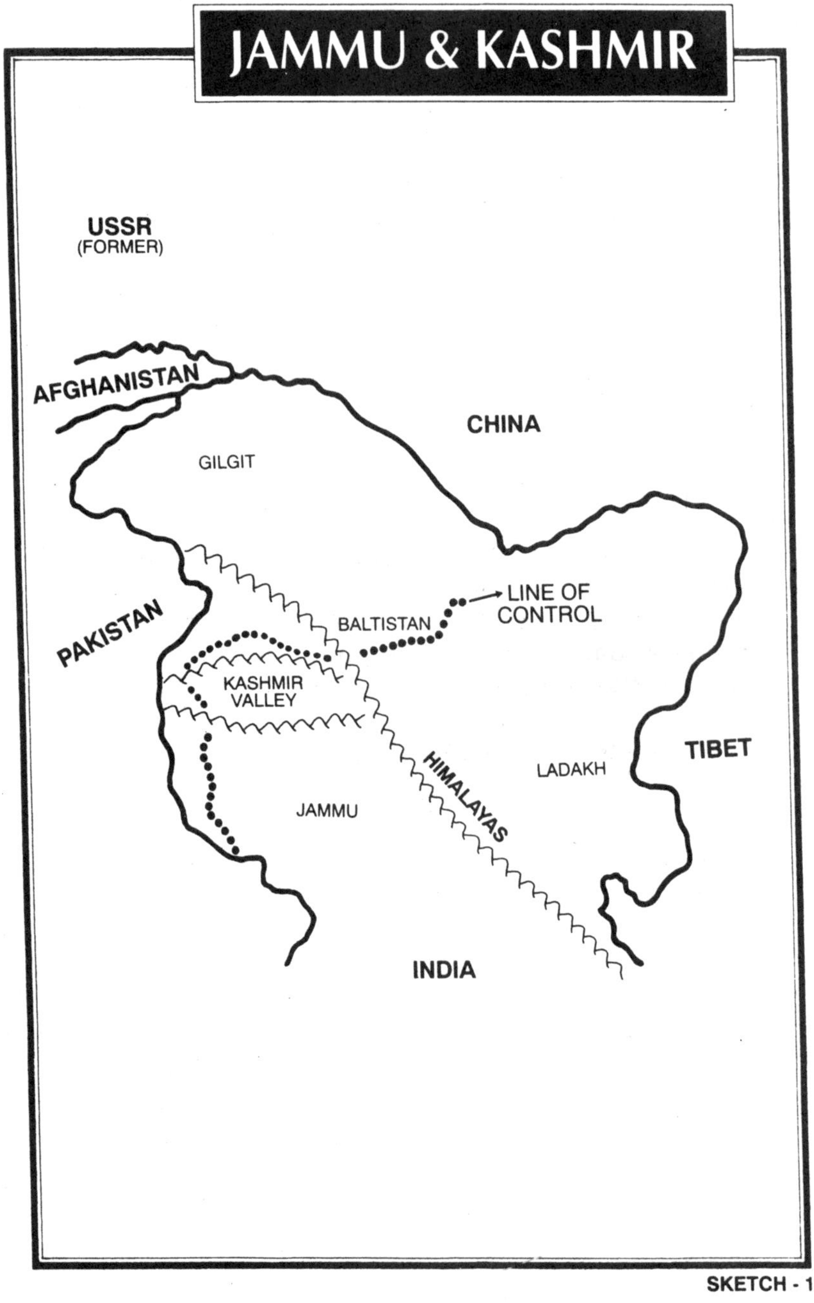
JAMMU & KASHMIR
USSR
(FORMER)
AFGHANISTAN
CHINA
GILGIT
PAKISTAN
BALTISTAN
LINE OF
CONTROL
KASHMIR
VALLEY
HIMALAYAS
TIBET
LADAKH
JAMMU
INDIA

SKETCH - 1

The Three Heroes Who Saved

LADAKH with

THE DALAI LAMA

18 March 1997

Colonel Prithi Chand MVC, The Dalai Lama, Brigadier Sher Jung Thapa, MVC, Colonel Chhewang Rinchen, double MVC, SM.

Brigadier Sher Jung Thapa

Colonel Prithi Chand

Colonel Chhewang Rinchen

Foreword

For centuries Ladakh was a part of the Tibetan history and its terrain an extension of Western Tibet. Therefore, the Tibetans and the Ladakhis share many things in common in their culture and in their way of life.

In this book, `Pakistan's Criminal Folly in Kashmir', Lieut. General (Retd.) M.L. Chibber has narrated the complete story of how Ladakh was defended from being captured by the invaders from the west fifty years ago. It is the story of a few dedicated men who rose to great heights of bravery. The bravery shown by Brigadier Sher Jung Chand, Colonel Prithi Chand, Colonel Rinchen, Engineer Sonam Norbu and Subedar Bhim Chand is highly admirable. I applaud the author for his painstaking research.

It is extremely important that the story or stories of the sacrifices and valour shown by exceptional and dedicated men and women should be told over and over again. Such accounts will inspire and encourage people in general and specially the young to strive for higher goals in life.

Ladakh today is one of the symbols of an ancient civilization that once flourished in the Himalayan region. Some of the ancient Buddhist monasteries located in Ladakh continue to function in utmost peace, tranquillity and freedom. What is most encouraging is that, even today, the Ladakhis continue to keep alive their traditional way of life and deeply cherish human values such as truth, love, righteousness, and non-violence. It is my hope that the good human values that exist in Ladakh will help in promoting harmony and peace in this region and beyond.

Dalai Lama

Preface

After working for Indo-Pakistan reconciliation for over ten years, I realise how *truth* can prove to be a great healer in human affairs. Tibet could have been saved from being captured by China in the early fifties if Indians had done their duty to help a threatened friend and neighbour. Unfortunately India failed in its *Dharma* and we are still paying a heavy price for that dereliction of duty.

I also felt that the great tragedy of partition of India in 1947 was essentially due to a clash of egos of some leaders who were more concerned with power and pelf than the welfare of the people. While everyone suffered by the tragedy of partition, the Muslim community has been its worst victim. Ultimately it was fractured into three nation states; the largest segment is in India, the second in Bangladesh, and the third in Pakistan. Partition is now a fact of history. It cannot and must not now be undone, but its ill-effects can be considerably mitigated by objective analysis of the background and the *truth* of the tragedy.

The communal frenzy following the partition turned men into animals. The herculean effort to save Ladakh from being the victim of this madness was undertaken by a few selfless men. It is essentially the story of the `three - musketeers' who rose to incredible heights of heroism. Their struggle was but a small facet of this tragedy, but an important one to understand as to why did the Kashmir problem arise at all.

It was in 1984 that I first met Colonel Prithi Chand, MVC, at Manali to listen to his fascinating story. I later met Brigadier Sher Jung Thapa, MVC, at Dharamsala and then Brigadier Ghansara Singh who was the Governor of Gilgit at the time of partition. It is from the memories and materials supplied by these men and the many libraries which I consulted that it was possible to put this story together. My grateful thanks to them all. I also like to thank Lt. Gen. Ram Kumar Gaur who has spent long years in Ladakh, for his ready assistance in putting this book together.

I was fortunate to meet an old friend Lt. Gen. Sir James Wilson in London. While talking to him about Indo-Pakistan reconciliation, he offered to let me read the draft chapters of his yet unpublished memoirs dealing with the partition period when he was in undivided India. As Military Assistant to General Douglas Gracy, the Commander-in-Chief of Pakistan soon after partition, he had a ringside seat to observe the roles of Pakistan and India in Kashmir. This enabled me to appreciate the *truth* of the tragedy of partition through the eyes of an impartial but interested and knowledgeable observer and friend of both the countries. My grateful thanks to him.

Mr P.K. Raghupathy, my life long friend, came forward to assist in editing the first script to give this book some coherence. Havildar Clerk B.S. Venkatramana Sharma painstakingly typed and retyped the chapters to make the final version ready. Havildar Som Raj of the Regimental History Cell did his cheerful best to take care of the paper-littered office with selfless love. My sincere thanks to all of them.

The famous artist Arul Raj converted some shabby and crumpled photographs into black and white sketches. These lend considerable visual realism to the contents of this book. My greatful thanks to Arul Raj.

It would not have been possible to produce this book but for the unstinted support of Major General B.A. Kariappa, the Colonel of J&K LI, Colonel R.E. Williams and indeed everyone in the Regiment. My grateful thanks to all. A special word of thanks to Colonel SNS Gurung (Retd.) of J&K LI living at Dharamsala who, with the help of Army authorities, arranged an audience of the three stalwarts of this book with the Dalai Lama.

It was with some hesitation that I approached His Holiness The Dalai Lama with a request to write the Foreword for this book dealing with a war. It is a mark of his commitment to peace that he readily agreed to do so to highlight the culture of peace, love, righteousness and truthfulness of the people of this bastion of Buddhist culture. I shall be ever grateful to this noble laureate and apostle of peace.

And finally, a word about the underlying hope in this humble endeavour. India and Pakistan will do well to remember that *truth* ultimately prevails:

> "By Time, verily man is in loss, except such as have faith, and do righteous deeds, and in mutual teaching of Haq (Truth) and patience and constancy"
>
> \- Sura 103

> "Sathyam - eva - Jayathe" - Truth always triumphs.
>
> \- Upanishads

The basic *truth* is that mankind is on march towards the unity of man, global economy and earth citizenship. A man of infinite wisdom has already articulated the blue print for this new age waiting - to - be - born. In just four lines he has distilled the essence of Quran Sharif; indeed of all the faiths and philosophies that have gripped the minds of men since the dawn of history:

> "There is only one nation, the nation of humanity;
> there is only one religion, the religion of love;
> there is only one language; the language of the heart,
> there is only one God, and he is omnipresent"*

Indians and Pakistanis owe it to their children and grand children to give up their hurts and hates and work towards reconciliation. Once this happens, Kashmir will become a bridge rather than a battle ground between India and Pakistan.

M.L. Chibber

*Sathya Sai Baba who spent a life time in a mosque is nowoperating from a global centre to promote human values of truth, love, right conduct and equanimity. He is the Chancellor of Sathya Sai Baba University at Puttaparthy near Bangalore, India

List of Photographs

List of Maps

CONTENTS

Colonel and Mrs. Prithi Chand in their lovely home near Manali in 1984. Colonel Prithi Chand triggerred the entire effort to save Ladakh

CHAPTER 1

Introduction

"In February 1948, Major Prithi Chand... led a small band of volunteers in mid-winter across the Zojila pass (in the Himalayas) in a snow blizzard... arrived at Leh... with indomitable courage held the enemy's advance by adopting Guerilla tactics... posterity will sing the praise of this young and brave officer." Thus reads the citation for the award of Maha Vir Chakra to Prithi Chand who saved Ladakh in 1948.

This gallant officer, now turning eighty in 1997 and his charming Gorkha wife, Rukamani, live on the outskirts of Manali. They own a small orchard. He is almost a forgotten hero, but there is laughter in their home. Rukamani is wary of the old man going out for parties. She complains in Gorkhali with a giggle "*Tunna Bhaera Aunchha*" (he comes home roaring drunk), Prithi Chand parries with equal delight that "Potatoes that my wife eats weigh more than the liquor I drink. She is a Potato addict." Guests are welcome in their home with great warmth. I and my wife called on them in August 1984. Their lovely flower beds are lined not with bricks but hundreds of empty beer bottles!!

"What prompted you to volunteer to go across the Himalayas on this mad-cap venture?" I asked Prithi Chand. The old man reflected deeply for a while, to recall the events that took place nearly four decades ago and

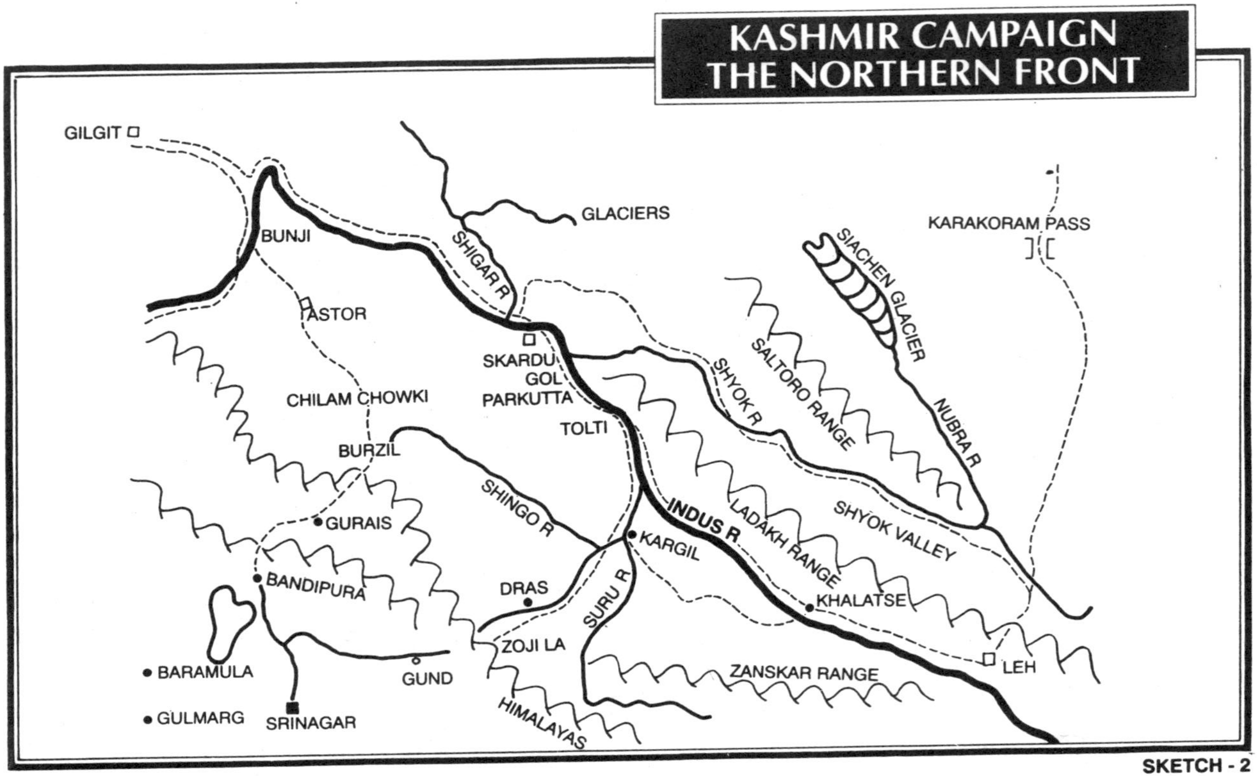
KASHMIR CAMPAIGN
THE NORTHERN FRONT
GILGIT
GLACIERS
KARAKORAM PASS
BUNJI
SHIGAR R
SIACHEN GLACIER
ASTOR
SKARDU
GOL
PARKUTTA
SALTORO RANGE
SHYOK R
CHILAM CHOWKI
TOLTI
NUBRA R
BURZIL
SHINGO R
INDUS R
LADAKH RANGE
SHYOK VALLEY
GURAIS
KARGIL
BANDIPURA
DRAS
SURU R
KHALATSE
ZOJI LA
LEH
BARAMULA
GUND
ZANSKAR RANGE
GULMARG
SRINAGAR
HIMALAYAS
SKETCH - 2

answered: "When I reached Srinagar with my Battalion in November 1947 to fight the Pakistani raiders, I learnt from local Ladakhis that most of the monasteries and well-to-do families in Leh had packed up their valuables, rare manuscripts, silver and gold statues and were getting ready to flee into Western Tibet. I was extremely upset to hear this distressing news. That night I saw my Guru, the Lama of Hemis Monastery, in my dream. He reminded me of the promises made to him in 1937 when he visited Lahaul, that I would protect his monastery, if ever it was threatened."

This book is the story of Major Prithi Chand who accomplished the impossible. There were only fifteen soldiers who volunteered to go with him on this historic mission; but for them, Ladakh would have fallen into Pakistani hands.

"Where do you belong to?" my wife enquired from Prithi Chand. The old man replied, "I belong to Lahaul which now is a part of Himachal Pradesh, but used to be a part of Kulu under the Sikhs before the British came."

My wife, who is a medical doctor, had travelled extensively with me in Ladakh, Zanskar, Lahaul and Spiti valley and had studied people of this region. Perhaps, out of intuition, she again questioned the old man, "Well, your family might have lived in Lahaul, but where do you actually belong to?".

Colonel Prithi Chand paused for a while, scratched his head, gave a hearty laugh and came out with a most fascinating story about his origin.

"I wonder how you guessed that I do not belong to a blue blood Lahauli family. I am amazed at your insight. Well, my ancestors, in the old days, belonged to the Pal Dynasty of Bengal. Many centuries ago, they migrated from Bengal and settled down in Kangra. They established two principalities of Chhota Bengal and Bada Bengal which still exist not very far from Mandi.

One of my adventurous ancestors, named Neel Pal, crossed over the Dhaula Dhar range which separates Lahaul from Kangra, Kulu and Manali. He married the daughter of the Raja of Lahaul and settled down there. The Raja belonged to the family of the great Tibetan Emperor, Tsrong Chem Ganbo, whose domain extended well into China, Mongolia, Ladakh, Lahaul and Spiti.

"My great grandfather was adopted as legal heir to the kingdom. The family adopted Buddhism when Lahaul was under the rule of the Rajas of Ladakh and took on the Ikshwaku caste of Lord Buddha. This caste in Tibet and Ladakh is called 'Guram Shingpa', meaning sugar-cane. During the period Lahaul was under the Ladakhi kings, our ancestors adopted Tibetan names. However, when Lahaul was annexed by the Raja of Kulu, we re-adopted Hindu names in addition to our Tibetan names, but retained our religion as Buddhism. For example, my Hindu name is Prithi Chand and my Tibetan name is Sonam Dawa. In Lahaul, we have a mixed Hindu and Buddhist culture as well as religion. Our gods and goddesses are common and our religious ceremonies are also common. So are our birth, marriage, and death ceremonies. We respect Buddhist Lamas and Hindu saints alike."

At this stage, Colonel and Mrs Prithi Chand took us to their prayer room. Goddess Durga, the deity of Mrs. Prithi Chand and Lord Buddha, that of the Colonel, adorn the room. The Colonel pulled out, some of his rare scriptures that had not been opened for decades. Written on thick black paper in golden letters and wrapped in silk, these rare family treasures are at least 500 years old. The Tibetan script looks very different, but we discovered to our amazement that phonetically it is exactly like the Sanskrit (Devnagri) script.

Prithi Chand was born on 1 January 1911, at Khangsar in Lahaul. His father, the late Rai Bahadur Thakur Amar Chand,

Raees-e-Azam, was then the Wazir of Lahaul. The title of Wazir had been bestowed on the ancestors of the family as a hereditary right with magisterial and administrative powers. This was during the reign of the Rajas of Ladakh and continued under the Rajas of Kulu and later under the British rule.

During the First World War, Thakur Amar Chand raised a volunteer force of two hundred men from Lahaul for the Mesopotamian Expeditionary Force. He himself volunteered to lead the group and was given the honorary rank of a Jamadar (now called Naib Subedar). After the War when they returned to Lahaul, the Government of India conferred the title of Rai Bahadur on Thakur Amar Chand, in recognition of his services, during the War. He was also granted 10 *murabbas* of land (250 acres) in the district of Montgomery in Western Punjab, now in Pakistan. Prithi Chand's father expired in 1921 when he was hardly 10 years old. His mother also died the same year and the eldest brother, Thakur Abhay Chand took over the duties of the Wazir of Lahaul. After passing Class 4 in a primary school in Lahaul, Prithi Chand was sent to Kulu government high school where he passed his matric examination in 1929. He then went to Shri Pratap College, Srinagar, for higher education. There he struck friendship with one Sonam Norbu of Ladakh who was destined to accompany Prithi Chand to save Ladakh in 1948. The studies had progressed for just three months, when he received a telegram to return home. On arrival, he found that his eldest brother had lost his mental balance. The middle brother, Thakur Pratap Chand, had to take over the duties of Wazir and Prithi Chand, perforce, had to discontinue his studies to look after the family farms and trade.

Prithi Chand's elder brother had joined 11 Dogra (TA) of the Territorial Army at Jullundur Cantt., and he was granted an Indian Territorial Force commission. Inspired by his brother

Prithi Chand also joined this Battalion as a Sepoy and in 1936, was promoted to the rank of Jamadar. He served in that capacity till 1939, when he was granted a commission and became an officer. The Territorial Army in those days used to undergo training for three months in a year, and for the rest of the time Prithi Chand would look after the family business and farms in Lahaul.

In 1936 Prithi Chand was elected as the President of Lahaul Wool Traders' Association. The Lahaulis purchased wool and pashmina from Tibetans and sold the same to traders from the plains, including Dhariwal Woollen Mills. With energetic efforts, Prithi Chand was able to raise the price of wool from Rs.15/- per maund to Rs.35/- per maund and was, thus, able not only to save the traders from suffering losses, but even to earn some profit instead. Seeing his performance, he was also selected as the Chairman of the Kuth Growers Association. Kuth is a root herb grown in high altitude areas. Its oil is exported to France for perfumes. The root was also exported to China for its medicinal and aphrodisiac qualities. He continued these activities till 1939 when World War II broke out.

The majority of the Lahaulis are Buddhists. The incarnate Lama of Hemis Monastery, Stag Tsang Rimpoche, was the Guru of Prithi Chand's family. In 1937 he paid a visit to Lahaul to bid farewell to all his followers. He explained that the visit would be his last trip because he was to leave this world by the next year. It was during this visit that he asked Prithi Chand to promise him to protect the sanctity of his monastery in case of a danger to its security. Prithi Chand gave his word, but had no inkling at all as to what was in the mind of the Lama. It was only in November 1947, when he saw him in his dream, that he realised the significance of the promise.

In 1939 Prithi Chand's Territorial Army Battalion was embodied: with it he saw service in various places in North

West Frontier Province where there was a threat of Russian invasion.

As a young Army Officer, 2/Lt. Prithi Chand was a most eligible bachelor in the region. During a short leave in Dharamsala, he lost his heart to a young and shy Gorkha girl, Rukamani. She was the daughter of a gallant Gorkha belonging to the 1st Gorkha Rifles. The old man had won a Military Cross and a Military Medal during the First World War. Fortunately for Prithi Chand, a family friend, Subedar Major Kalu Ram Thapa, IDSM, of Dharamsala, came forward to arrange the marriage. They took the vows on 4 November, 1940. Prithi Chand and Rukamani are so much devoted to each other and have had a most happy married life even though their separations have been long due to Prithi Chand being frequently away on active service. They have no children of their own, but have an adopted son. "It was only in the last few years before retirement that we had the pleasure of living together in family stations," recalls the Colonel. Their retired life has been extremely happy and homely.

After the War, Prithi Chand's Battalion was amalgamated with the 2 Dogra Regiment which was taken prisoner at Singapore. While in Japanese captivity, most of the personnel of this battalion joined the Indian National Army. As a consequence, only about 100 officers and men of the unit were retained in the Army to form a nucleus when the Battalion was reactivated after the war. The bulk of the manpower was provided by Major Prithi Chand's battalion which had its origin as a Territorial Army unit. During 1946 and 1947, Prithi Chand with his new unit was involved in internal security in the Punjab. There he witnessed the holocaust which took place at the time of partition of India. And yet there were numerous occasions when humanism could not be demeaned by the savage passions of the time.

Prithi Chand recalls this period with a certain amount of sadness, but he also has a vivid memory of the positive side of human nature. "I saw Muslims who gave protection and shelter to Hindus and Sikhs in West Punjab at great risk to their own lives. Similarly, Hindus and Sikhs gave protection to Muslims in East Punjab. Before the arrival of my Rifle Company, the Muslim Deputy Commissioner, a Haji, faced an armed mob who had come to plunder and massacre Hindus and Sikhs in the town. He persuaded them to return by saying that he was a Haji and would not allow innocent people to be killed. I saw a similar incident in Jagraon Tehsil in East Punjab where many Hindus and Sikhs came forward to protect the Muslim refugees and gave them food, transport and cash before they were evacuated."

An event which greatly influenced Prithi Chand and, perhaps, was in his sub-conscious when he volunteered to cross the Himalayas in the winter of 1947-48. In October 1947, while involved in the evacuation of refugees from Adampur near Jullundur, he had an opportunity to meet Pandit Jawaharlal Nehru who was on a visit to the area. He had heard Pandit Nehru in 1929 at the Congress party meeting at Lahore and later in 1942 at Kulu and Manali. But in October 1947 India was a free country and there was totally different environment all around. Panditji got hold of the few officers who were present at the airfield to receive him and said that the honour and the security of the country was in their hands. They should do everything possible to protect independent India. "These words said by Panditji still ring in my ears and have always carried a message for me in the execution of my duties." It is, indeed, amazing how leaders with vision enthuse people to make Herculean efforts for the sake of the country. Pandit Nehru made a lasting impact on Prithi Chand. After escorting the last convoy of Muslim refugees from Jullundur to Lahore, Prithi Chand requested for some leave to visit his wife at Dharamsala. "My wife had no information about my whereabouts. My bank accounts were left behind in Rawalpindi in Pakistan and she had no money at all. I arrived at Dharamsala on leave on 1 November, 1947 and we were planning to visit Kulu and Manali in the next few days. However, on the 4th, I received a wireless message from my unit through 1 Gorkha Rifles Regimental Centre at Dharamsala to report immediately at Pathankot. On reaching there, I was despatched to Srinagar as my Battalion had already been airlifted from Jullundur. We were involved in severe fighting with the Pakistani raiders on the outskirts of Srinagar. By the end of the month, we were in full control of the situation and my Battalion was concentrated at Baramula."

One day, while visiting Srinagar, Prithi Chand ran into Mr. Norbu of Ladakh, his old friend from the college days when they studied in Srinagar. Norbu was at that time a Divisional Engineer in the Kashmir PWD. He mentioned to Prithi Chand that it was not safe at Srinagar, and so he had sent his family away to Ladakh. But, unfortunately, Ladakh also was being threatened. It was this chance meeting between Prithi Chand and Norbu which triggered off Prithi Chand's commitment to protect Ladakh.

That night Prithi Chand went to sleep a bit late and slept uneasily. Suddenly he saw his Guru in a dream who reminded Prithi Chand of his promise to protect the Hemis Monastery and then the Guru disappeared. Prithi Chand sat up with a start with sweat on his forehead. What promise? When? Where? He had forgotten the incident of 1937. Slowly the memory came back and then Prithi Chand was like a dynamo. The theme of this book is to narrate the story of the three main actors who saved Ladakh.

Soon after the cease fire in Jammu and Kashmir in 1949, Prime Minister Jawaharlal Nehru visited the State and went to see the troops in the frontline. All available officers in and near Srinagar gathered in the Srinagar Club to listen the Prime Minister. General Thimmayya, the Commander of 19 Infantry

Division which conducted the operation in the Valley (originally named Sri Division), was showing the Prime Minister around. After a long and taxing day they returned in time for the address, but it was necessary to give some time to the Prime Minister to change his dust-covered clothes and take some rest before meeting the gathered officers. General Thimmayya took the opportunity of addressing the officers and narrated the role played by the 19 Infantry Division during the war. Second Lieutenant SNS Gurung who later commanded the 12 Jammu and Kashmir Light Infantry vividly remembers that address. It is relevant to record General Thimmayya's words in relation to saving of Ladakh :

"My strategy to save Ladakh was to hold on to Skardu at all costs, so that Pakistani forces may be prevented from reaching Kargil and Leh. Fortunately, I had the right man in Skardu to fulfil this mission. No words can describe the gallantry and leadership of Lieutenant Colonel Sher Jung Thapa who held on to Skardu with hardly 250 men for six long months. It is one of the longest sieges in the annals of war. While ordering him to defend Skardu to the last man and last round, I had promised to send him reinforcement and supplies; unfortunately neither could reach Skardu. I also tried to air-drop supplies and ammunition, but much of it fell outside his defences. Colonel Thapa then asked me not to air drop any more rations or ammunition as these were merely helping the enemy surrounding him. They held on even when they were on half and quarter daily rations. At the end of six months, when he completely ran out of rations and ammunition I ordered him to surrender. My general staff officer Colonel Siri Ram Oberai gave this order to the gallant officer on radio in August 1948. Thapa's response is etched on my mind and I can never forget it. He said: "I know that I cannot hold out without rations and ammunitions. General Thimmayya has failed me; I know the fate I and my troops will meet after surrendering to the enemy. Please convey to General

Thimmayya that he has not fulfilled his promise. I cannot do anything now against the enemy, but I will certainly take revenge in my next life." It is officers of this stamp who make great armies and great nations."

It is noteworthy that Thapa continued to hold the Skardu bastion even after the Pakistani force, in a brilliant 'right hook' operation, by-passed Skardu from the South through most rugged country and captured Zojila, Dras and Kargil during the month of May 1948. Thapa's concern proved right.

All his Sikh troops were murdered after surrender. The only Sikh who escaped this fate was Sepoy Kalyan Singh who was Thapa's orderly. He now lives in Jammu and invariably touches Thapa's feet whenever he visits Jammu, for saving his life. Simultaneously, strong Pakistani columns by-passed Skardu on the Northern side of river Indus to reach Leh where another gallant officer Major Prithi Chand was raising and training a guerilla force (later to become 7 J&K Militia) and getting an airfield constructed.

As pressure developed on Leh, Prithi Chand started sending urgent signals to Sri Division for reinforcements by air because he had got the landing strip at Leh ready with energetic efforts of his engineer friend Sonam Norbu and herculean work by the local population. When nothing happened he sent a personal signal to General Thimmayya about the breach of promise for air reinforcement alleging that troops and guerillas had lost confidence in their officers' promises of help and were ripe for desertion. He added: "Had no promises been made and forgotten, morale would not have suffered so much". General Thimmayya recalled these events and went on :

"The problem was that no one had flown and landed a Dakota at 11,000 ft above sea level, and consequently the Army and Airforce authorities at Delhi were unwilling to let Dakotas fly to Leh. I wanted to defend Leh at any cost. So, I thought it was best to ignore the "higher authorities". I called Air Commodore Mehr Singh for a drink. We discussed the grave situation and I asked him if he could fly to Leh. He said, "Of course, yes". "When?", I enquired and Baba (the nick name of this gallant airman) replied, "tomorrow". So the die was cast. I told Baba that I would fly with him. We carried some ammunition boxes in the aircraft. On reaching Leh we circled over the airfield and could see Prithi Chand and others virtually galloping on their ponies to the landing strip. We landed on 24 May '48 and gave the ammunition to Prithi Chand and told him to hold on till we could send air reinforcements by air. On return I wanted our people at Delhi to allocate the necessary air effort but received the stock answer 'Dakotas cannot land at Leh'. When I told them that I had just returned after landing there, they would not believe it."

We are now ready to recount in detail the heroic deeds of the gallant men who saved Ladakh :

- Lt. Col. (later Brigadier) Sher Jang Thapa, Maha Vir Chakra, at Skardu.
- Major (later Colonel) Prithi Chand, Maha Vir Chakra, at Leh.
- Nb. Sub. (later Colonel) Rinchen, Maha Vir Chakra and Bar and Sena Medal and Subedar Bhim Chand, Vir Chakra, in Shyok Valley.

In order to provide a backdrop to the unique role played by these heroes, it is necessary to take a look at the following two important aspects :-

- The drama of accession of the State of Jammu and Kashmir to India.
- The geography and history of Ladakh and its culture.

After discussing the above two features, we would be in a position to appreciate how Ladakh was saved by the single-minded resolve of men who rose to great heights of leadership to protect a territory which in size is larger than forty-five member states of the United Nations.

CHAPTER 2

The Drama of Accession of Jammu and Kashmir to India

"The tribal invasion was a criminal folly which sealed the gate of Kashmir"[18].

BACKGROUND

To understand the drama of accession it is necessary to briefly survey the history of the State.

In 1947, the State of Jammu and Kashmir was made up of two geographic regions divided by the great Himalayan Range (See Map 1). To the south lay the territories of Kashmir valley and Jammu. To the north of the range lay the three distinct areas of Ladakh in the east, Baltistan in the middle and Gilgit in the west.

From time immemorial the 'Paradise on Earth', Kashmir valley which forms the heart of the State, has attracted the eyes of poets, painters, monarchs, mountaineers, tourists,